Matthew L.

Matthew
The Gospel of Promised Blessings

LEADER GUIDE

Abingdon Press | Nashville

Matthew

The Gospel of Promised Blessings
Leader Guide

978-1-7910-3016-2

Cover Image: James B. Janknegt (b. 1953), *World's Smallest Seed*, 2011, Oil on Canvas, 40 x 30 inch, https://www.bcartfarm.com/.

Contents

Introduction

In *Matthew: The Gospel of Promised Blessings*, Dr. Matthew Skinner introduces or re-introduces his readers to "one of the most influential Christian writings ever produced." By turns familiar and frustrating, comforting and challenging, delightful and demanding, Matthew's Gospel confronts us with a visionary Jesus who calls for and will settle for nothing less than the complete transformation of human life so that it aligns with what Jesus usually calls "the kingdom of heaven."

This Leader Guide is designed to help small groups engage Matthew's Gospel using Skinner's book as an expert and trustworthy companion. Its six sessions correspond to the chapters of Skinner's book. Rather than present a start-to-finish commentary, Skinner groups several passages in each chapter thematically:

Session 1: Promised Blessings

Session 2: Promised Judgment

Session 3: A Vision for the Church and World

Session 4: Participating as Disciples

Session 5: Conflicts and Criticisms

Session 6: Taking Matthew Seriously Today

Each session contains the following elements to draw from as you plan six in-person, virtual, or hybrid sessions:

- Session Objectives
- Biblical Foundations: Scripture texts for the session, in the New Revised Standard Version Updated Edition.
- Before Your Session: Tips to help you prepare a productive session.
- Starting Your Session: Discussion questions intended to "warm up" your group for fruitful discussion.
- Book Discussion Questions: Recruit one or more volunteers to read each of the listed Scripture passages aloud, then discuss the passage using some or all of the questions provided. You likely will not be able or want to use all the questions in every session, so feel free to pick and choose based on your group's interests, leaving room for the Spirit to lead your discussion!
- Closing Your Session: A focused discussion to help participants move from reflection in the session to action beyond it.
- Opening and Closing Prayers

Thank you for leading your group in this study of Matthew's Gospel. May your study bring you all to a closer relationship with him whom Matthew calls Emmanuel, God-With-Us (Matthew 1:21), and who pledges to be with his church even to the end of this age (28:20).

Promised Blessings

Session Objectives

This session will help participants:

- Ponder how Jesus's pronouncements of blessing in Matthew 5:1-12 challenge commonly accepted criteria of satisfaction and success.
- Articulate and evaluate their understanding of "faith" in light of Jesus's promises to those "of little faith" in 6:30-33.
- Draw ethical implications from Jesus's parable of workers in a vineyard (20:1-16) about human dignity and wholeness.
- Reconsider their experiences of providing care to others as sacramental encounters with Jesus, in light of his parable of the "sheep and goats" (25:31-46).

Biblical Foundations

When Jesus saw the crowds, he went up the mountain, and after he sat down, his disciples came to him. And he began to speak and taught them, saying:

"Blessed are the poor in spirit, for theirs is the kingdom of heaven.

"Blessed are those who mourn, for they will be comforted.

"Blessed are the meek, for they will inherit the earth.

"Blessed are those who hunger and thirst for righteousness, for they will be filled.

"Blessed are the merciful, for they will receive mercy.

"Blessed are the pure in heart, for they will see God.

"Blessed are the peacemakers, for they will be called children of God.

"Blessed are those who are persecuted for the sake of righteousness, for theirs is the kingdom of heaven.

"Blessed are you when people revile you and persecute you and utter all kinds of evil against you falsely on my account. Rejoice and be glad, for your reward is great in heaven, for in the same way they persecuted the prophets who were before you."

(Matthew 5:1-12)

"But if God so clothes the grass of the field, which is alive today and tomorrow is thrown into the oven, will he not much more clothe you—you of little faith? Therefore do not worry, saying, 'What will we eat?' or 'What will we drink?' or 'What will we wear?' For it is the gentiles who seek all these things, and indeed your heavenly Father knows that you need all these things. But seek first the kingdom of God and his righteousness, and all these things will be given to you as well."

(Matthew 6:30-33)

"For the kingdom of heaven is like a landowner who went out early in the morning to hire laborers for his vineyard. After agreeing with the laborers for a denarius for the day, he sent them into his vineyard. When he went out about nine o'clock, he saw others standing idle in the marketplace, and he

said to them, 'You also go into the vineyard, and I will pay you whatever is right.'...When those hired about five o'clock came, each of them received a denarius. Now when the first came, they thought they would receive more; but each of them also received a denarius. And when they received it, they grumbled against the landowner, saying, 'These last worked only one hour, and you have made them equal to us who have borne the burden of the day and the scorching heat.' But he replied to one of them, 'Friend, I am doing you no wrong; did you not agree with me for a denarius? Take what belongs to you and go; I choose to give to this last the same as I give to you. Am I not allowed to do what I choose with what belongs to me? Or are you envious because I am generous?' So the last will be first, and the first will be last."

(Matthew 20:1-4, 9-16)

"When the Son of Man comes in his glory and all the angels with him, then he will sit on the throne of his glory. All the nations will be gathered before him, and he will separate people one from another as a shepherd separates the sheep from the goats, and he will put the sheep at his right hand and the goats at the left. Then the king will say to those at his right hand, 'Come, you who are blessed by my Father, inherit the kingdom prepared for you from the foundation of the world, for I was hungry and you gave me food, I was thirsty and you gave me something to drink, I was a stranger and you welcomed me, I was naked and you gave me clothing, I was sick and you took care of me, I was in prison and you visited me.' Then the righteous will answer him, 'Lord, when was it that we saw you hungry and gave you food or thirsty and gave you something to drink? And when was it that we saw you a stranger and welcomed you or naked and gave you clothing? And when was it that we saw you sick or in prison and visited you?' And the king will answer them, 'Truly I tell you, just as you did it to one of the least of these brothers and sisters of mine, you did it to me.'"

(Matthew 25:31-40)

Before Your Session

- Carefully and prayerfully read this session's Biblical Foundations, more than once. Consult a trusted study Bible and/or commentaries for additional background information.

- Carefully read the introduction and chapter 1 of Skinner's book. Note topics about which you have questions or want to research further before your session.
- *You will need*: Bibles for in-person participants and/or screen slides prepared with Scripture texts for sharing (note the translation you use); newsprint or a markerboard and markers (for in-person sessions).
- If using the DVD or streaming video, preview the session 1 video segment. Choose the best time in your session plan for viewing it.

Starting Your Session

Welcome participants. Tell them why you are excited to study *Matthew: The Gospel of Promised Blessings* with them. Invite volunteers to speak briefly about why they are interested in this study and what they hope to gain from it.

Invite participants to open their Bibles to Matthew's Gospel. Set a timer for five minutes (or so, depending on time constraints), during which participants should skim the Gospel. When time runs out, invite volunteers to call out anything they noticed as they skimmed—favorite (or not-so-favorite) verses, famous stories, and so on. Write responses on newsprint or markerboard. Discuss:

- Based on your quick review, what topics and ideas seem most important to Matthew?
- How would you describe Matthew's tone, and why?
- What, if anything, surprised you most as you skimmed Matthew?

Offer these observations from Skinner's book:

- Most Bible scholars date Matthew's Gospel to 80–100 CE—at least a decade after Rome destroyed the Temple in

Jerusalem, and at least five decades after Jesus's death and resurrection.

- Matthew generally follows Mark as its source, but about 25 percent of its material is unique, including the story of the magi and King Herod (Matthew 2), the Sermon on the Mount (Matthew 5–7), and several well-known parables (such as 25:31-46).

- Matthew has been called both the "most Jewish" Gospel because of its quotations of and interest in Jewish Scripture (the Christian Old Testament) and the "most anti-Jewish" because of its often-caricatured portrayal of Jewish religious leaders and others who disagree with, oppose, or reject Jesus.

- In Matthew, Jesus is depicted as an urgent, impassioned, intense, and sometimes angry visionary who announces the "kingdom of heaven" (Matthew's preferred language for "kingdom of God")—"a state of affairs in which God's intentions have sway."

- Jesus's intensity in Matthew manifests itself, in part, in demands for decisive choices and in more talk of judgment and punishment than in most New Testament books.

Opening Prayer

Righteous God, who inspired your servant whom we know as Matthew to tell the story of Jesus for a troubled community in a troubled time: Inspire our study of his work in these sessions, that your same Spirit may strengthen us to more fully embrace and embody Jesus's vision of the kingdom of heaven. Amen.

Watch Session Video

Watch the session 1 video segment together. Discuss:

- Which of Skinner's statements most interested, intrigued, surprised, or confused you? Why?
- What questions does this video segment raise for you?

Book Discussion Questions

Recruit one or more volunteers to read each of the listed Scripture passages aloud, then discuss the passage using some or all of the questions provided. You likely will not be able or want to use all the questions, so feel free to pick and choose based on your group's interests.

Matthew 5:1-12

- Why does Matthew make a lengthy sermon the first of Jesus's major public events in this Gospel?
- What does the word *blessed* make you think or feel? How do you define it?
- Skinner says blessed, in Matthew's Greek, means something closer to "satisfied" or "unburdened." What are some situations in which you feel or have felt most satisfied and unburdened? How, if at all, do those experiences influence the way in which you hear Jesus's pronouncements of blessing?
- Skinner points out that Jesus doesn't define any of the eight categories of people who are "blessed." How do you respond to Skinner's descriptions of these groups? With which of these groups, if any, do you most and/or least identify, and why?
- The Roman-controlled Mediterranean world was "an agonistic society"—one "marked by competition," in which "social status, power, and privilege matter in every

social interaction." To what extent would you describe your society today as agonistic, and why?

- How do Jesus's pronouncements of blessing challenge accepted standards, in our own society, of satisfaction and success?
- To whom would (and does) Jesus address statements of blessing today?
- Skinner notes Jesus's statements here are declarations, not commands. Yet for nearly 2,000 years, Christian and non-Christian thinkers alike have drawn ethical conclusions from these declarations. What are some specific ways you and your congregation might need to change values in light of Jesus's declarations?

Matthew 6:30-33

- What is your definition of faith?
- If pressed, would you say you have a little or a lot of faith? Why?
- Who is a person you've known (or known of) whom you would say had great faith? Why?
- Skinner says Jesus refers to all or most of us when he talks about those "of little faith." Do you agree? Why or why not?
- Skinner suggests the English translation "trust" most closely matches what Jesus means by "faith." In your everyday life, in what and in whom do you trust the most? How does this trust show itself in what you do?
- Who places great trust in you? How do you know? How does the experience of someone placing trust and faith in you inform your experience of placing trust and faith in God?

- What promise does Jesus make to those "of little faith" in these verses? How do you understand this promise? Do you trust it? Why or why not?
- "As God's ways come to pass, we know how to use God's gifts to ensure that everyone receives care." Were someone unfamiliar with your congregation to examine the ways in which you use God's gifts to care for others, what would they conclude about your level of trust and faith in God? Why?

Matthew 20:1-16

- If you were to give this parable a fresh and original title, what would you title it, and why?
- Have you ever been surprised, or even offended, when someone was treated as your equal? What happened?
- How would you describe the landowner as a character?
- Skinner suggests the people hired last and latest in the day were those who most needed work and struggled most to find it. How does this suggestion influence your reactions to the story? Who are the equivalent of these late-day workers in your own community?
- Skinner also suggests readers interpret the wages in this story as "suggestive and partial, not a comprehensive depiction of how dignity is recognized or bestowed." What are some other ways you and your congregation work to bestow dignity on those to whom social systems deny it?
- "When it comes to the wholeness God offers, God is determined not to leave anyone out." Who is missing from your congregation's embodiment of the wholeness God offers to and desires for humanity? What are you doing, or could you do, to include them?

Matthew 25:31-46

- If you were to give this parable a fresh and original title, what would you title it, and why?

- Skinner notes domesticated sheep and goats were hard for those who didn't work with livestock to tell apart in Jesus's day. Why is this fact significant for understanding and interpreting Jesus's parable?

- What do you make of the fact that neither the "sheep" nor the "goats" are aware they saw and responded to Jesus—or didn't (25:37-39, 44)?

- What's the difference between helping someone and going out of one's way to help someone in "desperate conditions"? When, if ever, have you done so? Given the righteous don't remember times they did so, does recalling and discussing such a time in your life somehow undermine its significance? Why or why not?

- When, if ever, has someone gone out of their way to demonstrate compassion to you?

- What connections can you draw between this parable and Jesus's pronouncements of blessings in Matthew 5:1-12?

- Skinner notes this parable is the last Jesus tells before his crucifixion. How, if at all, does this fact influence the way you hear and react to the parable?

- What ethical implications, if any, do you draw from Skinner's statement that being kind to people in desperate conditions can be a sacramental encounter with Jesus?

- Why does Skinner argue it is important to read Jesus's parable as a parable about Jesus's presence in the wider world, beyond the church's boundaries? How does or how could such an understanding shape your and your congregation's interactions with that wider world?

Closing Your Session

Christians believe, as Matthew did, that Jesus was *more* than a visionary—but he was not *less*. As Skinner notes, visionaries can sometimes express frustration and anger, as Jesus does in Matthew; they also call people, in great compassion and great urgency, to embrace their vision.

Ask participants to think of other people—past or present, whom they personally know or not—whom they would call visionaries. Discuss:

- How and why do these individuals challenge conventional wisdom, accepted norms, and the status quo?
- How they are like and unlike Jesus, as Matthew presents him?
- What visionary challenges have you raised, or would you be willing to raise, as a consequence of following the visionary Jesus?

Closing Prayer

Jesus, Son of Man who will come in glory: You promise we can meet you now, in and among those you call the least of your family. Strengthen us to labor in your vineyard as long and as vigorously as we can, rejoicing in your generosity, trusting in your grace, and always seeking first your reign. Amen.

Promised Judgment

Session Objectives

This session will help participants:

- Confront and discuss some commonly held negative opinions about Christians and judgment.
- Consider John the Baptist's message (Matthew 3:1-12) in the context of Matthew's interest in telling the truth about immorality and injustice.
- Examine the purpose of Matthew's stark dualism, as illustrated in Jesus's parable of two houses (7:24-27), as an expression of the ancient teaching device of "the two ways."
- Draw conclusions from Jesus's parable of the dragnet (13:47-50) about how his followers should approach evil and dangerous things.

- Put real-life situations in dialogue with promises of judgment and grace in Matthew's Gospel.

Biblical Foundations

In those days John the Baptist appeared in the wilderness of Judea, proclaiming, "Repent, for the kingdom of heaven has come near." ...

But when he saw many of the Pharisees and Sadducees coming for his baptism, he said to them, "You brood of vipers! Who warned you to flee from the coming wrath? Therefore, bear fruit worthy of repentance, and do not presume to say to yourselves, 'We have Abraham as our ancestor,' for I tell you, God is able from these stones to raise up children to Abraham. Even now the ax is lying at the root of the trees; therefore every tree that does not bear good fruit will be cut down and thrown into the fire.

"I baptize you with water for repentance, but the one who is coming after me is more powerful than I, and I am not worthy to carry his sandals. He will baptize you with the Holy Spirit and fire. His winnowing fork is in his hand, and he will clear his threshing floor and will gather his wheat into the granary, but the chaff he will burn with unquenchable fire."

(Matthew 3:1-2, 7-12)

"Everyone, then, who hears these words of mine and acts on them will be like a wise man who built his house on rock. The rain fell, the floods came, and the winds blew and beat on that house, but it did not fall because it had been founded on rock. And everyone who hears these words of mine and does not act on them will be like a foolish man who built his house on sand. The rain fell, and the floods came, and the winds blew and beat against that house, and it fell—and great was its fall!"

(Matthew 7:24-27)

"Again, the kingdom of heaven is like a net that was thrown into the sea and caught fish of every kind; when it was full, they drew it ashore, sat down, and put the good into baskets but threw out the bad. So it will be at the end of the age. The angels will come out and separate the evil from the righteous and throw them into the furnace of fire, where there will be weeping and gnashing of teeth."

(Matthew 13:47-50)

Before Your Session

- Carefully and prayerfully read this session's Biblical Foundations, more than once. Consult a trusted study Bible and/or commentaries for additional background information.
- Carefully read chapter 2 of Skinner's book. Note topics about which you have questions or want to research further before your session.
- *You will need*: Bibles for in-person participants and/or screen slides prepared with Scripture texts for sharing (note the translation you use); newsprint or a markerboard and markers (for in-person sessions).
- If using the DVD or streaming video, preview the session 2 video segment. Choose the best time in your session plan for viewing it.
- *Optional* (for in-person sessions): recent newspapers and magazines.

Starting Your Session

Welcome participants. Ask them, by show of hands, whether they strongly agree, agree, disagree, or strongly disagree—give no "neutral" option—with each of these statements:

- Christians enjoy determining what is and isn't sinful.
- Christians are too intolerant of and judgmental toward other people.
- Christians are hypocrites.

(If meeting via videoconference or in hybrid format, you could prepare a poll in which participants can click their responses to each statement.)

After tallying the results, briefly discuss each statement, inviting volunteers to talk about why they responded as they did, as well as what the statements made them think and feel. Tell participants non-Christians often strongly agree with each of the statements, and often with good reason.

Ask: "Have you, personally, ever been accused with these statements, or ones like them? How did you respond?"

Tell participants Skinner, in chapter 2 of his book, suggests Christians reading Matthew often shy away from this Gospel's talk of judgment in order to avoid such accusations. However, he also suggests such talk is unavoidable and important for understanding Matthew's presentation of Jesus and needs to be viewed together with what Jesus says about God's love and acceptance.

Opening Prayer

High and holy God, sovereign over all: We gather to hear, study, and respond to your words of grace and judgment. By your Spirit, help us hold your mercy and compassion together with your justice and holiness, that we may tell the truth about you and your righteous will for us and for the world, following in the way of our Lord and Savior Jesus. Amen.

Watch Session Video

Watch the session 2 video segment together. Discuss:

- Which of Skinner's statements most interested, intrigued, surprised, or confused you? Why?
- What questions does this video segment raise for you?

Book Discussion Questions

Recruit one or more volunteers to read each of the listed Scripture passages aloud, then discuss the passage using some or all of the questions provided. You likely will not be able or want to use all the questions, so feel free to pick and choose based on your group's interests.

Matthew 3:1-12

- What do you think and feel when you hear calls to "repent"?

- As Skinner points out, Matthew's description of John (3:4; compare Mark 1:6) evokes scriptural traditions about Elijah. Read 1 Kings 18:20-21, 36-40; 2 Kings 1:5-8; Malachi 4:1-5. What might Matthew want to accomplish by associating John with Elijah (as did Jesus; see Matthew 17:10-13)?

- What does John's preaching and baptizing activity call on God's people to choose for and against? How are these choices reflected in your congregation's or tradition's baptismal practices?

- Skinner stresses that confession and repentance are more about telling the truth than about feeling sorry and apologizing for wrongs. Why is truth-telling the necessary first step in repairing broken relationships with others and with God, and in repairing this broken world?

- Why does John reserve his most urgent, harshest words for religious leaders (verses 7-10)?

- When, in your knowledge or direct experience, have religious leaders' power and influence made religion burdensome, or even harmful or abusive, to those they are supposed to guide and care for? What causes religious leaders, across denominations and faith traditions, to be prone to such behavior? What can be done to make things better?

- How does remembering that John and the Pharisees and Sadducees (let alone Jesus and his first followers) were all Jewish believers help Christian readers avoid interpreting John's message as a condemnation of Judaism?

- Skinner suggests most of his students, and maybe most of his readers, resemble the Pharisees more than other characters in the Gospels, because they are religious insiders. How can we religious insiders see and tell difficult but necessary truths about ourselves from a new perspective?

- "John talks the way people talk when they're out of patience and have grown utterly sick of injustice and wickedness." Who have you heard talk in the same way? When and why do you talk this way? How can and do people who talk this way translate such talk into positive, constructive action?

- John does "more than hurl warnings; he also issues invitations." How do you and your congregation balance warnings and invitations in your worship and your witness?

Matthew 7:24–27

- Skinner notes that Matthew's Gospel often adopts a harshly dualistic worldview. How does this saying of Jesus reflect that dualism?

- How do you see and experience—and, perhaps, consciously or unconsciously contribute to—a dualistic worldview in your life?

- Read Deuteronomy 30:19; Jeremiah 21:8; Psalm 1:6. How does Jesus's dualistic language reflect the ancient teaching device of "the two ways" seen in these and other Scriptures? What does this teaching device hope to accomplish? How effective do you find it, and why?

- What point is Jesus trying to make in his story about the two builders and their houses? Why does this point seem so urgent to Jesus? How urgent does it seem to you? Why?

- Why does Skinner say taking the images in these verses as a warning about final judgment is a mistake? Do you agree?

- When and how have you experienced the difference between "building" your life on "rock" and "sand"?

- How do we discern which situations and moments call for Jesus's and the Hebrew Scriptures' kind of urgent dualism, and which don't?

Matthew 13:47–50

- Skinner says Jesus's parables, like those other ancient teachers told, use images familiar to their original audience in unfamiliar ways. They are comparisons that "jolt" audiences into new perspectives. What parables of Jesus, from any of the Gospels, do you remember the most, and why?

- Read Matthew 13:10-17, 34-35. According to these passages, why did Jesus teach using parables? How do these passages confirm or challenge your understanding of his parables? How do these passages reflect the dualism Skinner has already highlighted in Matthew's Gospel?

- Unlike some of his other parables, Jesus's parable of the dragnet is, says Skinner, "not too exciting." What are your immediate reactions to this parable?

- How does understanding the dragnet as gathering more than fish affect your understanding of the parable? What ethical conclusions can you draw from the premise that the Kingdom is somehow "a universal, comprehensive reckoning"?

- If angels, rather than we, are responsible for sorting "the evil from the righteous"—the decaying from the desirable, the bad from the good—"at the end of the age" (verse 49), what are our responsibilities regarding what is evil and what is righteous right now?

- Skinner suggests the parable means the Kingdom's arrival will eliminate dangerous and corrupt "things," rather than "people." Why is this distinction significant? How can it shape our attitudes toward, interactions with, and conclusions drawn about people who are physically or morally dangerous, to us or to others, today?

- Skinner encourages readers to avoid overemphasizing the imagery of punishment and destruction with which this parable (and others—for example, 13:42; 25:46) ends. How do you react to such imagery? How important do you think it is to understanding Jesus's message, and why? What dangers accompany stressing such imagery too much—and/or too little?

- Skinner imagines how different Christianity would be were the parable of the dragnet the only parable we had from Jesus. How would having only one of the more memorable or "exciting" parables we mentioned earlier distort our understanding of and relationship with God and Jesus?

Closing Your Session

Read aloud from Skinner's book:

> If the world is a harsh place, as a quick scan of today's
> news probably confirms, then divine love without
> judgment just gives people company in their unending
> misery...[and] divine judgment without love will end
> up consuming all of us....Jesus's promises of judgment
> don't cancel God's graciousness....They mean we leave
> the judgment up to God, trusting that divine love
> extends to us and even to our enemies....

Encourage participants to spend a few minutes in that scan of the news Skinner mentions, either by checking reputable news sites on their devices and/or by skimming recent newspapers and magazines. Ask participants to select a news item that somehow speaks to them about the importance of divine judgment and/or graciousness. Invite several volunteers to speak briefly about the item they choose, and how they think it relates to the topics of God's judgment and God's grace. This activity isn't intended to produce a litany of bad news for bad news' sake, but to help participants imagine how Jesus's promises of both judgment and grace in Matthew speak to concrete situations today.

Closing Prayer

Jesus our Teacher who baptizes with the Holy Spirit and fire: Help us secure our lives on the rock-solid foundation of your word, telling your truth and choosing your way that we may persist in righteousness, until the day you send your angels to heal us and the world of all evil with God's own unshakable love. Amen.

A Vision for the Church and World

Session Objectives

This session will help participants:

- Appreciate Jesus as a "dreamer" with a specific vision for safe and harmonious human community.
- Articulate Jesus's approach to Torah (the Law) and apply it to the church today.
- Identify ways in which they and their congregation do or could care for "harassed and helpless" (9:36), vulnerable people.
- Understand what Jesus meant by "humility" and compare and contrast his understanding with common (mis) understandings of humility today.

- Talk about ways Jesus's promised presence with the church shapes their congregation's practices of conflict resolution and forgiveness.

Biblical Foundations

"Do not think that I have come to abolish the Law or the Prophets; I have come not to abolish but to fulfill. For truly I tell you, until heaven and earth pass away, not one letter, not one stroke of a letter, will pass from the law until all is accomplished. Therefore, whoever breaks one of the least of these commandments and teaches others to do the same will be called least in the kingdom of heaven, but whoever does them and teaches them will be called great in the kingdom of heaven. For I tell you, unless your righteousness exceeds that of the scribes and Pharisees, you will never enter the kingdom of heaven.

(Matthew 5:17-20)

Then Jesus went about all the cities and villages, teaching in their synagogues and proclaiming the good news of the kingdom and curing every disease and every sickness. When he saw the crowds, he had compassion for them because they were harassed and helpless, like sheep without a shepherd. Then he said to his disciples, "The harvest is plentiful, but the laborers are few; therefore ask the Lord of the harvest to send out laborers into his harvest."...

These twelve Jesus sent out with the following instructions: "Do not take a road leading to gentiles, and do not enter a Samaritan town, but go rather to the lost sheep of the house of Israel. As you go, proclaim the good news, 'The kingdom of heaven has come near.' Cure the sick; raise the dead; cleanse those with a skin disease; cast out demons. You received without payment; give without payment. Take no gold, or silver, or copper in your belts, no bag for your journey, or two tunics, or sandals, or a staff, for laborers deserve their food. Whatever town or village you enter, find out who in it is worthy, and stay there until you leave."

(Matthew 9:35-38; 10:5-11)

At that time the disciples came to Jesus and asked, "Who is the greatest in the kingdom of heaven?" He called a child, whom he put among them, and said, "Truly I tell you, unless you change and become like children, you will never enter the kingdom of heaven. Whoever becomes humble like this child is the greatest in the kingdom of heaven. Whoever welcomes one such child in my name welcomes me."

(Matthew 18:1-5)

Then Peter came and said to him, "Lord, if my brother or sister sins against me, how often should I forgive? As many as seven times?" Jesus said to him, "Not seven times, but, I tell you, seventy-seven times.

"For this reason the kingdom of heaven may be compared to a king who wished to settle accounts with his slaves. When he began the reckoning, one who owed him ten thousand talents was brought to him, and, as he could not pay, the lord ordered him to be sold, together with his wife and children and all his possessions and payment to be made. So the slave fell on his knees before him, saying, 'Have patience with me, and I will pay you everything.' And out of pity for him, the lord of that slave released him and forgave him the debt. But that same slave, as he went out, came upon one of his fellow slaves who owed him a hundred denarii, and seizing him by the throat he said, 'Pay what you owe.' Then his fellow slave fell down and pleaded with him, 'Have patience with me, and I will pay you.' But he refused; then he went and threw him into prison until he would pay the debt. When his fellow slaves saw what had happened, they were greatly distressed, and they went and reported to their lord all that had taken place. Then his lord summoned him and said to him, 'You wicked slave! I forgave you all that debt because you pleaded with me. Should you not have had mercy on your fellow slave, as I had mercy on you?' And in anger his lord handed him over to be tortured until he would pay his entire debt. So my heavenly Father will also do to every one of you, if you do not forgive your brother or sister from your heart."

(Matthew 18:21-35)

Before Your Session

- Carefully and prayerfully read this session's Biblical Foundations, more than once. Consult a trusted study Bible and/or commentaries for additional background information.

- Carefully read chapter 3 of Skinner's book. Note topics about which you have questions or want to research further before your session.
- *You will need*: Bibles for in-person participants and/or screen slides prepared with Scripture texts for sharing (note the translation you use); newsprint or a markerboard and markers (for in-person sessions).
- If using the DVD or streaming video, preview the session 3 video segment. Choose the best time in your session plan for viewing it.
- *Optional*: Find a video or audio recording of (portions of) Martin Luther King Jr.'s "I Have a Dream" speech (August 28, 1963) to watch or listen to as a group.

Starting Your Session

Welcome participants. Ask participants what they know about Martin Luther King Jr.'s "I Have a Dream" speech. If necessary, refer to Skinner's summary of it in chapter 3. Optional: Watch or listen to a recording of (portions of) the speech. Discuss:

- What did King mean by calling his vision for the US a "dream"?
- How does calling a vision of sweeping change like King's a "dream" help and/or hinder it from becoming reality?
- Is being called "a dreamer" a compliment? A criticism? Something else entirely? Why? Have you ever been called "a dreamer"?
- Skinner cites New Testament scholar Mary Hinkle Shore's reference to Jesus's Sermon on the Mount as Jesus's "I Have a Dream" speech. How accurate or helpful do you find the comparison, and why?

Tell participants Skinner calls Jesus, as Matthew presents him, "a dreamer." In this session, your group will explore Jesus's dream for human community as he intends for it to take concrete shape in his community, his church.

Opening Prayer

God Who Sees, may your Spirit look on us with grace as we turn again to Matthew's Gospel, seeking fresh insight and new understanding into the words and work of your Son, Jesus. Lead us to read and talk together with mutual respect, patience, humility, and compassion. May this time of study help us more fully share Jesus's dream for his church and the world. Amen.

Watch Session Video

Watch the session 3 video segment together. Discuss:

- Which of Skinner's statements most interested, intrigued, surprised, or confused you? Why?
- What questions does this video segment raise for you?

Book Discussion Questions

Recruit one or more volunteers to read each of the listed Scripture passages aloud, then discuss the passage using some or all of the questions provided. You likely will not be able or want to use all the questions, so feel free to pick and choose based on your group's interests.

Matthew 5:17–20, 48; 6:1

- What does Jesus mean by saying he has come "to fulfill" the Law and the Prophets (5:17)?
- As Skinner explains, Jesus, like other Jews, saw Torah ("the Law") as a way for people to live a life that "aligns

with God's best intentions for humanity." How similar or
dissimilar is this attitude to attitudes about the Law in your
Christian tradition? To your own attitudes—if any—about
the Law?

- While "Pharisee" is often an unfortunate synonym for
  sanctimonious hypocrisy in modern English, Skinner
  points out people in Jesus's day did not question the
  Pharisees' devotion to God's righteousness. What does
  Jesus mean when he says his followers' righteousness must
  exceed that of the Pharisees? Were he speaking in today's
  society, whose righteousness would he say his followers'
  righteousness must surpass? Why?

- Skinner says Jesus enlarges the scope of various
  commandments in Torah (5:21-47). How so? What does
  Jesus achieve, or hope to achieve, by setting the bar of
  Torah observance for his community as high as he does?

- Does this section of the Sermon on the Mount confirm
  or challenge the commonly held idea that Jesus rejected or
  wanted to reform his Jewish faith? How so?

- Skinner states the common element in Jesus's teaching
  about the Torah's commandments is Jesus's call for his
  followers to "go out of [their] way" to care for each other.
  When has someone gone "out of their way" to care for
  you? When have you gone "out of your way" to care for
  someone else?

- According to Skinner, how does Jesus's idea of being
  "perfect" (5:48) differ from our common understanding of
  perfection? How does this distinction make you feel about
  the standard to which Jesus is calling his followers?

- Jesus identifies almsgiving, prayer, and fasting in private
  as specific ways in which his followers should "practice

righteousness." Which of these practices do you and your congregation practice? In what other ways do you practice righteousness? How do you keep these practices from becoming mere performances?

Matthew 9:35–38; 10:5–11

- Skinner says the work Jesus calls his community to do is a rebuke to cruelty and apathy that leave people "harassed and helpless" (9:36). Who are the "harassed and helpless" in your community? What are you and your congregation doing to connect with, care for, and nourish them?

- Matthew says Jesus sees the harassed, helpless crowd as "sheep without a shepherd." What metaphor might you use to describe such people today?

- What do Jesus's instructions to his apostles in Matthew 10 say, directly and indirectly, about his initial priorities for his church? How well would you say your congregation's priorities align with these, and why?

- Jesus prepares his apostles to expect hardship, rejection, and even persecution (10:14-25). What promises does Jesus make to help them? What's the difference between expecting difficulty in Jesus's service and actively courting it? How do we distinguish actual persecution from unfavorable circumstances or mere inconvenience?

- Skinner points out that the apostles are sent to carry Jesus's own ministry forward. They are to do the things Jesus has already done, and when others welcome them, they are welcoming him (see 10:40-42). How easy or difficult is it for you to think of what you and your congregation doing as Jesus's own ministry? Why?

- Why do you think Matthew doesn't report the results of the apostles' missionary journey (in contrast to Luke 10:17-20)? Skinner suggests Matthew's narrative choice avoids triumphalism, adding, "History teaches us how dangerous a conceited church can be." What examples can you think of? How present a danger do you think triumphalism is for today's church? For your congregation? Why?

Matthew 18:1-14

- How was childhood in the ancient world, as Skinner describes it, like and unlike childhood in various parts of today's world?
- What does Jesus's choice of a child to illustrate who is "greatest in the kingdom of heaven" (18:1) tell us about that kingdom?
- How do you respond to humility and powerlessness as hallmarks of God's kingdom? How can exhortations to humility be used (and how have they been used) in ways that harm people and undermine God's values and priorities? What can and must individual believers and congregations do to prevent such harm?
- What is Jesus's vivid and violent imagery in verses 6-9 meant to communicate?
- Who have you known or known of who demonstrates dedication to protecting the vulnerable like that of the shepherd in Jesus's parable (verses 12-13)? How do you and your congregation demonstrate such dedication?
- What safeguards does your congregation have in place for protecting children and any vulnerable people?

Matthew 18:15-35

- What kind of situations are Jesus's instructions in verses 15-17 meant to address? What kind are they not intended to address? How can we tell the difference?

- Does your congregation follow Jesus's words as a "template" for resolving conflicts? Why or why not? What do you know about healthy conflict resolution that Jesus simply doesn't address here?

- What does treating a repeat, unrepentant offender like "a gentile and a tax collector" (verse 17) look like today, especially considering how Jesus dealt with Gentiles, tax collectors, and other "sinners"?

- Why does Jesus's parable in verses 23-34 stress the enormously exaggerated difference between what the first enslaved person owed his master, and what his fellow enslaved person owed him?

- "Jesus's parable reads like a tragedy," writes Skinner. Do you agree? Why or why not? How does this parable help us understand God's kingdom?

- What insights does viewing sin as financial debt, as this parable does, offer? What are the limitations of this image? What other images help you think about what sin is, and how to forgive it?

- For what reasons does Skinner say forgiveness isn't as easy as Christians usually make it sound? Do you agree? Why or why not?

- How does Jesus's promised presence among his followers (verse 20) shape the way your congregation deals with conflict and practices forgiveness?

Closing Your Session

Skinner points out that Jesus never says his church is the only place in which people will live out his values. Discuss:

- When and where have you experienced people outside the church embodying Jesus's values and vision?
- How do you and your congregation cooperate with others who live out Jesus's values, but do not do so in Jesus's name?
- If others beyond the church can and do live a life aligned with Jesus's dream for the world, why or how much should the church still matter to Christians and to the world?
- What can the church offer the world that other people and groups struggle to offer?

Closing Prayer

Jesus, our good and forgiving Shepherd: Strengthen us to share your righteous impatience and dissatisfaction with how far short we and our world fall of God's perfect will. Enable us to dream with you of a safe and harmonious life for all, and empower us, by your Spirit, to take what steps we can to make that dream a reality now. Amen.

Participating as Disciples

Session Objectives

This session will help participants:

- Appreciate Matthew's legal genealogy of Jesus in light of his Gospel's attention to the wide range of people with whom Jesus associates.
- Explore implications of Jesus's call of Matthew the tax collector for Christian work and worship today.
- Interpret Jesus's saying about his easy yoke and light burden (11:28-30) in language accessible to modern audiences.
- Glean insights from Matthew's reports of Jesus's healing ministry in 12:15-21 and 15:29-31 for Christian responses to pain and suffering today.

- Reflect on Jesus's commissioning of his disciples (28:16-20) as a pattern for discipleship today.

Biblical Foundations

As Jesus was walking along, he saw a man called Matthew sitting at the tax-collection station, and he said to him, "Follow me." And he got up and followed him.

And as he sat at dinner in the house, many tax collectors and sinners came and were sitting with Jesus and his disciples. When the Pharisees saw this, they said to his disciples, "Why does your teacher eat with tax collectors and sinners?" But when he heard this, he said, "Those who are well have no need of a physician, but those who are sick. Go and learn what this means, 'I desire mercy, not sacrifice.' For I have not come to call the righteous but sinners."

(Matthew 9:9-13)

"Come to me, all you who are weary and are carrying heavy burdens, and I will give you rest. Take my yoke upon you, and learn from me, for I am gentle and humble in heart, and you will find rest for your souls. For my yoke is easy, and my burden is light."

(Matthew 11:28-30)

When Jesus became aware of this, he departed. Many followed him, and he cured all of them, and he ordered them not to make him known. This was to fulfill what had been spoken through the prophet Isaiah:

"Here is my servant, whom I have chosen,
my beloved, with whom my soul is well pleased.
I will put my Spirit upon him,
and he will proclaim justice to the gentiles.
He will not wrangle or cry aloud,
nor will anyone hear his voice in the streets.
He will not break a bruised reed
or quench a smoldering wick
until he brings justice to victory.
And in his name the gentiles will hope."

(Matthew 12:15-21)

After Jesus had left that place, he passed along the Sea of Galilee, and he went up the mountain, where he sat down. Great crowds came to him, bringing with them the lame, the blind, the maimed, the mute, and many others. They put them at his feet, and he cured them, so that the crowd was amazed when they saw the mute speaking, the maimed whole, the lame walking, and the blind seeing. And they praised the God of Israel.

(Matthew 15:29-31)

Now the eleven disciples went to Galilee, to the mountain to which Jesus had directed them. When they saw him, they worshiped him, but they doubted. And Jesus came and said to them, "All authority in heaven and on earth has been given to me. Go therefore and make disciples of all nations, baptizing them in the name of the Father and of the Son and of the Holy Spirit and teaching them to obey everything that I have commanded you. And remember, I am with you always, to the end of the age."

(Matthew 28:16-20)

Before Your Session

- Carefully and prayerfully read this session's Biblical Foundations, more than once. Consult a trusted study Bible and/or commentaries for additional background information.

- Carefully read chapter 4 of Skinner's book. Note topics about which you have questions or want to research further before your session.

- *You will need*: Bibles for in-person participants and/or screen slides prepared with Scripture texts for sharing (note the translation you use); newsprint or a markerboard and markers (for in-person sessions).

- If using the DVD or streaming video, preview the session 4 video segment. Choose the best time in your session plan for viewing it.

Starting Your Session

Welcome participants. Discuss:

- How interesting or important do you find your genealogy, and why?
- Do you have any famous people in your family tree? Any non-famous but especially colorful characters? If so, who?
- Have you ever been surprised—pleasantly or unpleasantly—to discover something about your family history?

Ask participants to turn in their Bibles to Matthew 1. Have them skim 1:1-17 and call out any names they may recognize, and what they remember about those names. (If time allows and you have brave volunteers, recruit one or more to read the genealogy aloud.) Ask:

- Why do you think Matthew begins his Gospel with Jesus's legal genealogy?
- What significance do you find in Matthew's symmetrical, three-part arrangement of Jesus's genealogy (verse 17)?
- Skinner acknowledges the five women mentioned in Jesus's genealogy (Tamar, verse 3; Rahab, verse 5; Ruth, verse 5; Bathsheba, "the wife of Uriah," verse 6; Mary, verse 16); all have complicated stories but ought not be reduced to sexual scandals associated with them. What lessons about faithfulness, families, and God's purposes can we learn from these women?
- "God's blessings travel widely," writes Skinner. How, if at all, do you see your family history as a testimony to God's widely traveling blessings?

Tell participants this session will explore other stories in Matthew that, like the genealogy, demonstrate the width and breadth of the people God called to accompany and be accompanied by Jesus.

Opening Prayer

God of the ages: Thank you for gathering us again to read and respond to the written witness of the Gospel of Matthew. May our study, reflection, and discussion lead us to know our place more fully in the large company you have called to be saints in your Son's presence. We dare ask you to surprise us again with the good news of your mercy in Christ. Amen.

Watch Session Video

Watch the session 4 video segment together. Discuss:

- Which of Skinner's statements most interested, intrigued, surprised, or confused you? Why?
- What questions does this video segment raise for you?

Book Discussion Questions

Recruit one or more volunteers to read each of the listed Scripture passages aloud, then discuss the passage using some or all of the questions provided. You likely will not be able or want to use all the questions, so feel free to pick and choose based on your group's interests.

Matthew 9:9-13

- When you hear the word *sinners*, what kind of people come to mind? (*No naming individuals, please!*) What other labels do we use, perhaps when we are wanting to be polite and respectable, to dehumanize others in society? When, if ever, has a dehumanizing label been applied to you, and how did you respond?

- Why did people in Jesus's society generally hold tax collectors in disregard? What makes Jesus's choice of Matthew to follow him a surprise?

- Why did Jesus pay special attention to those on the margins of his society? How much attention would you say you and your congregation pay to people on the margins: too little? too much? just the right amount? Why?

- Have outsiders ever expressed surprise at who eats with you and/or your congregation?

- What does Jesus mean when he calls those to whom he is ministering "sick" (verse 12)? How does he treat their "sickness"?

- How effective do you think moral exhortation (or moral lecturing) is or can be in the service of the gospel?

- When, if ever, has someone given you "a dose of divine mercy" instead of a scolding? How did that mercy affect you? How, if at all, does it affect you still?

- Skinner notes that Jesus doesn't reject the "conventionally respectable"; he indicates his priorities are elsewhere. What hope should or could "conventionally respectable" people take from this fact? What warnings, if any?

- How can and do Christians today discern whether their "legal and liturgical categories" are animated by a spirit of mercy (verse 13)?

Matthew 11:28-30

- In Scripture, Skinner explains, a yoke can be a metaphor for either oppressive subjugation or obedience to God. What metaphors or images might Jesus use today to describe his "easy yoke"?

- Do you have mostly positive, mostly negative, or mixed associations with the idea of obedience? How does our society view obedience? How do these associations make Jesus's words easier or harder to understand, for Christians and for others?
- Skinner says he doesn't often experience discipleship as "easy" or convenient. What about you? If discipleship is often neither easy nor convenient, what does Jesus mean by calling his burden "light"?
- When have you, as Skinner has, experienced joy in discipleship?

Matthew 12:15-21

- "Crowds are faceless characters in narratives as in real life." When did you most recently find yourself in a crowd? What was the experience like? What's your most enjoyable memory of being in a crowd? Your least enjoyable?
- Why are many people following Jesus in this report about his ministry? Why does Jesus order them not to talk about him?
- What is the "this" of which Jesus becomes aware in verse 15 (see 12:1-14)? How does this context influence how you hear and understand this passage?
- Skinner says Jesus doesn't need to go looking for pain and suffering—they come to him. When was a time you responded to someone in pain and suffering who came to you? When was a time you did not respond? What accounted for the difference?
- Jesus is committed to healing people because he is compassionate. In what concrete actions do you and your

congregation's compassion for people in pain and suffering find expression?

- Matthew paraphrases Isaiah 42:1-4 to interpret Jesus's healing ministry. Why is Matthew concerned to show the continuity between Jesus and Israel's previous history with God? How would you respond to someone who said, "Isaiah must have been predicting Jesus"? How would you respond to someone who said, "Matthew is taking Isaiah's words completely out of context"?

- Who do you know, or know of, who has or gone about healing work in a silent, humble, gentle way (verses 19-20)?

- How can Christians today discern when following Jesus means working silently for those in pain and suffering, and when it means making some noise for the same people?

Matthew 15:29-31

- How is this summary of Jesus's healing ministry like and unlike the one in Matthew 12:15-21?

- How is Jesus's healing ministry, in Skinner's words, "a taste of a transformed existence"?

- Have you known of or personally experienced a physical healing you consider miraculous? If so, what happened? If not, do you believe such healings do or could occur? Why or why not?

- Where and when, if ever, have you encountered an assumption that physical infirmity is a sign of sinfulness or of God's disfavor? How did or do you respond to such an assumption?

- Do you agree with Skinner that presenting Jesus's healings as "symbols about sin and forgiveness" is problematic? Why or why not?

- How would you—or, perhaps, how have you—responded to someone who suggests physical healing is a reward for faithfulness?
- What does it mean to you that the crowd appears to be composed of Gentiles, since they praise "the God of Israel"?
- How, if at all, are you or your congregation engaged in the work of physical healing?

Matthew 28:16-20

- Why does Skinner claim Jesus sending his disciples to the "nations" or "Gentiles" is a "slightly predictable finale" to Matthew's Gospel? How has Matthew prepared his Gospel's readers for this expansion of the circle of Jesus's followers?
- The disciples who meet the risen Jesus in Galilee simultaneously worship and doubt him (verse 17). How much or little does this statement of contradiction mirror your own experience of faith?
- In some of the other Gospels' stories of Jesus's resurrection appearances, Jesus attempts to reassure doubting disciples. Why doesn't he do so in this story?
- How does Jesus's claim to all authority in heaven and on earth (verse 18) challenge claims to authority we encounter in the world and in the church today?
- How does, or how ought, Jesus's claim to all authority shape the church's priorities, values, and activities today?
- What specific activities does the risen Jesus tell his disciples to do? What form do these activities take in your and your congregation's activities?

- Why is Jesus's last word to his disciples in Matthew a word about his continuing presence with them?

Closing Your Session

Skinner points out that, in Matthew's Gospel, we rarely see Jesus interacting with his disciples one-on-one but often see him surrounded by a community of those who follow him. He writes that "following Jesus is a collective, cooperative endeavor." Discuss:

- What experiences of community have been most important to you in your awareness of Jesus's presence?
- How is the image of Jesus among a community a challenge and a corrective to a tendency to define ourselves primarily as individuals?
- What are some ways of following Jesus that Christians can only practice together, in community?
- In what collective, cooperative, and communal ways does your congregation seek to extend Jesus's mercy to each other and in the world?

Closing Prayer

Lord Jesus, who received all authority in heaven and earth: You choose to authorize us, works in progress though we are, to maximize your mercy in the world. May your Spirit strengthen us to respond to the pain and suffering we encounter, and to strive for all people's healing and wholeness, that the crowds around us may praise, not us, but the God of Israel. Amen.

Conflicts and Criticisms

Session Objectives

This session will help participants:

- Interpret Jesus's critiques of Pharisees in Matthew 23 as rejections of attitudes and behaviors to which anyone, especially religious people, may fall prey.
- Reflect on Jesus's parables of the wise and foolish young women (25:1-13) and the talents (25:14-30) as stories about faithful and unfaithful responses to opportunities for serving God.
- Evaluate Matthew's depiction of Pontius Pilate in light of both the historical record and patterns of predatory leadership in society.
- Relate Matthew's account of the first Easter to evidence of God's power to break down resistance to God's reign today.

Biblical Foundations

Then Jesus said to the crowds and to his disciples, "The scribes and the Pharisees sit on Moses's seat; therefore, do whatever they teach you and follow it, but do not do as they do, for they do not practice what they teach. They tie up heavy burdens, hard to bear, and lay them on the shoulders of others, but they themselves are unwilling to lift a finger to move them. They do all their deeds to be seen by others, for they make their phylacteries broad and their fringes long. They love to have the place of honor at banquets and the best seats in the synagogues and to be greeted with respect in the marketplaces and to have people call them rabbi. But you are not to be called rabbi, for you have one teacher, and you are all brothers and sisters. And call no one your father on earth, for you have one Father, the one in heaven. Nor are you to be called instructors, for you have one instructor, the Messiah. The greatest among you will be your servant. All who exalt themselves will be humbled, and all who humble themselves will be exalted."

(Matthew 23:1-12)

"Then the kingdom of heaven will be like this. Ten young women took their lamps and went to meet the bridegroom. Five of them were foolish, and five were wise. When the foolish took their lamps, they took no oil with them, but the wise took flasks of oil with their lamps. As the bridegroom was delayed, all of them became drowsy and slept. But at midnight there was a shout, 'Look! Here is the bridegroom! Come out to meet him.' Then all those young women got up and trimmed their lamps. The foolish said to the wise, 'Give us some of your oil, for our lamps are going out.' But the wise replied, 'No! there will not be enough for you and for us; you had better go to the dealers and buy some for yourselves.' And while they went to buy it, the bridegroom came, and those who were ready went with him into the wedding banquet, and the door was shut. Later the other young women came also, saying, 'Lord, lord, open to us.' But he replied, 'Truly I tell you, I do not know you.' Keep awake, therefore, for you know neither the day nor the hour."

(Matthew 25:1-13)

The governor again said to them, "Which of the two do you want me to release for you?" And they said, "Barabbas." Pilate said to them, "Then what should I do with Jesus who is called the Messiah?" All of them said, "Let him be crucified!" Then he asked, "Why, what evil has he done?" But they shouted all the more, "Let him be crucified!"

So when Pilate saw that he could do nothing but rather that a riot was beginning, he took some water and washed his hands before the crowd, saying, "I am innocent of this man's blood; see to it yourselves." Then the people as a whole answered, "His blood be on us and on our children!" So he released Barabbas for them, and after flogging Jesus he handed him over to be crucified.

(Matthew 27:21-26)

Before Your Session

- Carefully and prayerfully read this session's Biblical Foundations, more than once. Consult a trusted study Bible and/or commentaries for additional background information.
- Carefully read chapter 5 of Skinner's book. Note topics about which you have questions or want to research further before your session.
- *You will need*: Bibles for in-person participants and/or screen slides prepared with Scripture texts for sharing (note the translation you use); newsprint or a markerboard and markers (for in-person sessions).
- If using the DVD or streaming video, preview the session 5 video segment. Choose the best time in your session plan for viewing it.
- *Optional*: hymnals

Starting Your Session

Welcome participants. Ask and discuss one or more of these questions:

- When has someone accused you, or when have you accused yourself, of not "practicing what you preach"? How did you determine whether the charge was accurate, and what, if anything, did you do about it?

49

- When have you been caught unprepared by something for which you should have been prepared? How did you feel? What did you do?
- When was a time you were entrusted with someone else's valuable possessions or resources? Did you view how you handled that responsibility as a test of character? Why or why not?

Tell participants to keep their discussion of these issues in mind as your group reads and reflects on the Scriptures in today's session.

Opening Prayer

God of Israel, God and Father of our Lord Jesus Christ: Your Son's ministry among us sparked conflict between competing values, priorities, and visions for human life. As we study these stories of conflict, may the bond of your Spirit keep us united in faith, that we may all grow together as Jesus's faithful followers. Amen.

Watch Session Video

Watch the session 5 video segment together. Discuss:

- Which of Skinner's statements most interested, intrigued, surprised, or confused you? Why?
- What questions does this video segment raise for you?

Book Discussion Questions

Recruit one or more volunteers to read each of the listed Scripture passages aloud, then discuss the passage using some or all of the questions provided. You likely will not be able or want to use all the questions, so feel free to pick and choose based on your group's interests.

Matthew 23:1-15 (16-36)

- Broadly speaking, Jesus's several charges against Pharisees are all charges of hypocrisy. Why is hypocrisy a persistent problem in any religion?
- Skinner stresses that Matthew's depiction of Pharisees is one-sided and "absolutely negative." Why is caricaturing and demonizing those with whom we disagree unhelpful at best, dangerous at worst?
- How have Matthew's caricatures of Pharisees influenced nearly two thousand years of Christian attitudes toward Jewish people and Judaism? What are you and your congregation doing, or what could you do, to promote healthier and more faithful relationships between Jews and Christians today?
- Without defending Matthew's caricature of Pharisees, Skinner suggests reasons it had power for Matthew and his community. What are those reasons? What are healthier ways your congregation uses or could use to draw closer to Jesus, and navigate disagreements about how best to interpret and obey Scripture?
- Read Skinner's description of what history tells us about Pharisees' attitude toward observing Torah. Why does he say Pharisees did not believe in or practice "works righteousness"?
- What are some practices you and your congregation follow to live everyday life "with high regard for honoring God's holiness," as was the Pharisees' intent?

Matthew 25:1–13 (14–30)

- With whom are your sympathies in this parable: the wise young women? the foolish ones? the groom? Why?

- Why does the groom say he doesn't know the five foolish young women (verse 12; compare Matthew 7:21-23)?
- Why does Skinner say, "Christianity is a waiting religion"? What does this parable tell us about wise versus foolish ways to wait?
- When have you and your congregation done things that would be "wise" in a way this story would recognize? What about "foolish" things?
- Why does the master in Jesus's parable call the enslaved man who doesn't trade with the talent he was given "wicked and lazy" (verse 26)? How does the master's reaction confirm the enslaved man's opinion of him (verse 24)? Do you think the master's judgment of the man is fair? Why or why not?
- Skinner says the third enslaved man failed to embrace an opportunity. What is a grand opportunity you have not taken? What factors did you weigh, if any, when deciding whether to take it? Do you regret your decision? Why or why not?
- "These parables," Skinner writes, "are emphasizing the grand blessings Jesus gives his followers to spread around." What do you identify as Jesus's grand blessings? How have you and your congregation taken and created opportunities to spread them around?
- "We sometimes act...as if we can afford to offer only scarcity." When have you encountered this tendency in yourself? in your congregation? How do you combat a mindset of scarcity in your stewardship of God's blessings?

Matthew 27:15-26

- How does the historical record's depiction of Pontius Pilate, as summarized by Skinner, differ from the Pilate we see in Matthew's Gospel? Why is knowing about these differences important?

- Why does Skinner say Pilate had "virtually no choice but to crucify someone like Jesus"? How does the supposed choice Pilate sets before the crowd (verses 15-17) reinforce, rather than call into question, Pilate's and the Roman Empire's authority over their Judean subjects?

- Why do you think Matthew, alone among the evangelists, mentions the curious detail of Pilate's wife's dream (verse 19)?

- Why does Matthew want his audience to know about the leaders' influence over the crowd (verse 20)? When have you seen leaders mislead the people for whom they are responsible, including within religious communities?

- Read Deuteronomy 21:1-9. How does this passage provide significant background for Pilate's handwashing (Matthew 27:24)?

- Skinner notes Pilate wants to make the crowd complicit in his responsibility—"the art of a tyrant." Why is avoiding responsibility for one's decisions and actions a tyrannical "art"? What have been some of the hard decisions you've nevertheless taken responsibility for in your life?

- Commenting on the damage of anti-Jewish interpretations of verse 25 (which we will study closer in the last session), Skinner says whether Matthew intended to blame all Jewish people for Jesus's death "matters little." How important is it to distinguish between Matthew's original intent and his words' later impact? To what extent can we know Matthew's intent?

- "As Matthew depicts it, Jesus dies in a world harassed by predatory leadership." What actions do or could you and your congregation take against predatory leaders in church and society today?

Closing Your Session

Invite a volunteer to read Matthew 28:1-6 aloud. Read aloud from Skinner's book: "For Matthew, the resurrection of Jesus Christ...rebukes 'the way things are.'" Discuss:

- How does Matthew's uniquely dramatic account of the first Easter morning communicate God's challenge to the status quo?
- How does Matthew's Easter story point to the Resurrection as being about "a new quality of life with God"?
- Skinner states Matthew's Easter story tells us God can break "patterns of resistance" to God's reign—resistance from leaders, from institutions, and even from us ourselves. Where and how do you see God breaking down resistance to God's reign today?

Optional: Distribute hymnals and sing together an Easter hymn familiar to participants.

Closing Prayer

Risen and Living Christ, roll away our fear of living as joyful and generous citizens of your coming kingdom, even now: make us quick to take opportunities to share your blessings; slow to chastise those we do not see responding to you; steadfast in our refusal to be manipulated away from your priorities; and actively, patiently waiting for your return. Amen.

Taking Matthew Seriously Today

Session Objectives

This session will help participants:

- Evaluate the magi (Matthew 2:1-12) as outsiders who offer valuable insight into where and through whom God can be at work.
- Reflect on what Jesus's parables of the weeds among wheat (13:24-30) and the mustard tree (13:31-32) can teach about the kingdom of heaven and Jesus's intentions for his church.
- Interpret the blood libel of Matthew 27:25 in ways that seek to avoid perpetuating antisemitic and anti-Jewish stereotypes and hatred.

- Use the story of Peter walking on water with Jesus (14:28-32) as inspiration for taking further steps in faith, individually and as a congregation.

Biblical Foundations

In the time of King Herod, after Jesus was born in Bethlehem of Judea, magi from the east came to Jerusalem, asking, "Where is the child who has been born king of the Jews? For we observed his star in the east and have come to pay him homage." When King Herod heard this, he was frightened, and all Jerusalem with him, and calling together all the chief priests and scribes of the people, he inquired of them where the Messiah was to be born....

When they had heard the king, they set out, and there, ahead of them, went the star that they had seen in the east, until it stopped over the place where the child was. When they saw that the star had stopped, they were overwhelmed with joy. On entering the house, they saw the child with Mary his mother, and they knelt down and paid him homage. Then, opening their treasure chests, they offered him gifts of gold, frankincense, and myrrh. And having been warned in a dream not to return to Herod, they left for their own country by another road.

(Matthew 2:1-4, 7-12)

"And the slaves of the householder came and said to him, 'Master, did you not sow good seed in your field? Where, then, did these weeds come from?' He answered, 'An enemy has done this.' The slaves said to him, 'Then do you want us to go and gather them?' But he replied, 'No, for in gathering the weeds you would uproot the wheat along with them. Let both of them grow together until the harvest, and at harvest time I will tell the reapers, Collect the weeds first and bind them in bundles to be burned, but gather the wheat into my barn.' "

(Matthew 13:27-30)

He put before them another parable: "The kingdom of heaven is like a mustard seed that someone took and sowed in his field; it is the smallest of all the seeds, but when it has grown it is the greatest of shrubs and becomes a tree, so that the birds of the air come and make nests in its branches."

(Matthew 13:31-32)

Then the people as a whole answered, "His blood be on us and on our children!"

(Matthew 27:25)

Before Your Session

- Carefully and prayerfully read this session's Biblical Foundations, more than once. Consult a trusted study Bible and/or commentaries for additional background information.

- Carefully read chapter 6 and the Afterword of Skinner's book. Note topics about which you have questions or want to research further before your session.

- *You will need*: Bibles for in-person participants and/or screen slides prepared with Scripture texts for sharing (note the translation you use); newsprint or a markerboard and markers (for in-person sessions).

- If using the DVD or streaming video, preview the session 6 video segment. Choose the best time in your session plan for viewing it.

Starting Your Session

Welcome participants. Ask those who have attended previous sessions to reflect on one or two key "takeaways" they will remember from this study, or one or two questions they still have about Matthew's Gospel. Be ready to share at least one new thing you have learned or one question you still have after leading this study.

Opening Prayer

Holy God, as we gather to conclude this study of Matthew's Gospel, remind us that, in our lives as Jesus's disciples, our study of your Word and our striving to discern your will never cease. As we examine the few final texts in our study, show us how you examine us—not seeking out our faults, which you already know, but searching for our fruits of faithfulness. May our contemplation and conversation in this time together equip us to produce us the righteousness you seek, even as we trust in the righteousness of your Son, Jesus. Amen.

Watch Session Video

Watch the session 6 video segment together. Discuss:

- Which of Skinner's statements most interested, intrigued, surprised, or confused you? Why?
- What questions does this video segment raise for you?

Book Discussion Questions

Recruit one or more volunteers to read each of the listed Scripture passages aloud, then discuss the passage using some or all of the questions provided. You likely will not be able or want to use all the questions, so feel free to pick and choose based on your group's interests.

Matthew 2:1-12

- What do you think of when you think about the magi in the "Christmas story"?
- Why would Skinner want the magi in a movie of this story to "be a little funky"? What visual cues would mark someone as "not from around here" in your community? in your congregation?
- Skinner thinks the magi are examples of courage. How so? Do you agree? Why or why not?
- Why are King Herod "and all Jerusalem with him" (verse 3) afraid at the magi's report of the newborn "king

of the Jews" (verse 2)? How prominently is this aspect of Jesus's birth reflected in your and your congregation's Christmas observances?

- Skinner says the magi remind us "truth can come from unexpected sources." From what unexpected sources and unexpected people have you encountered truth—and how did you know?

- "Yes, theology matters," writes Skinner, yet "Jesus has so little to say in Matthew about exactly what he wants people to believe." Why do you think this is the case? How does the ratio of belief and action in your congregation match the ratio in Matthew's Gospel?

- How does or can attending to outsiders, as the magi were outsiders, help us stay focused on the welcome and mercy that characterized Jesus's ministry?

Matthew 13:24-30, 36-43

- Why does Skinner suggest Matthew's Gospel contains several stories, like this one, about sortings? Have you ever been part of a community concerned with identifying and separating truth from falsehood, good from bad? What happened?

- Skinner says the landowner in Jesus's parable shows "great wisdom" in allowing weeds and wheat to grow together. Why? Do you agree?

- According to Jesus's explanation of his parable (and it is one of the few he does explain), what does each element in the story represent? Which of these elements interests or perplexes you most? Why?

- How do you react to Jesus's fiery image of judgment (verse 42)? Why is it significant to note that Jesus says causes of sin (verse 41) will go into this furnace?

- Do you think this parable's emphasis on God as final judge encourages Jesus's church today to be more or less active in the face of today's evil? Why?

- "Especially in our modern times," Skinner writes, "congregations can be strong engines for advocacy and reform." When and how have you seen congregations act this way? How, specifically, is your congregation advocating against evil?

- How does your congregation make space for people who may need extra time and tending to grow spiritually? What extra time and tending do you think you could use to encourage your spiritual growth? How does or could this group and your congregation give that time and tending to each other?

Matthew 13:31-32

- As Skinner points out, the mustard seed isn't actually the smallest seed in nature, and mustard grows into a shrub, not a tree. How, if at all, do these facts influence your understanding of Jesus's parable?

- Read Ezekiel 17:22-24, which Skinner says Jesus's parable evokes. What similarities and differences between the two texts do you observe? How does one help you understand the other?

- Skinner suggests this parable encourages us to look in humble places for the kingdom of heaven. When do you believe you have glimpsed the Kingdom in humble circumstances?

- When have you or others you know or know of experienced the shelter and relief of the Kingdom in or through your congregation, as the nesting birds experience it in the mustard tree's branches?

- Skinner suggests calling the church a "family" is "problematic." Do you agree? Why or why not?
- What parts of an "ecosystem" designed to nourish life are firmly in place in your congregation? What parts may need strengthening, or may be missing altogether? What can and will your congregation do to address them?

Matthew 27:25

- What recent antisemitic or anti-Jewish incidents, if any, are you aware of in your community? your region? in the United States? Check your awareness against searching reputable and trustworthy news sources.
- Have you encountered the "Christ-killer" slur against Jewish people firsthand, or in literature, TV or film, or art?
- How can Christians today interpret Matthew 27:25 in ways that avoid placing blame for Jesus's death on all Jewish people, in all times and places?
- Skinner says this verse is Matthew's "subtle attempt" at pointing to the consequences for Jewish leaders of his day having rejected Jesus. Do you agree with his assessment? Why or why not?
- Skinner rejects the "theological insinuation" that the Jewish people "somehow got what they deserved" when Rome sacked Jerusalem and destroyed the Temple in the year 70 because "other parts of the Bible lead [him] to understand that God doesn't operate that way." What does the Bible as a whole lead you to think about this "insinuation," and why?
- As·problematic as it is and as violent as the history of its interpretation has been, Skinner doesn't want to cut this verse from the Bible—"we'd be tempted never to put

down our scissors." Yet we all probably have mental scissors we take to Scripture. How can we ensure we pay attention to troublesome, offensive verses and stories today— or should we make the effort to do so? What risks do we run engaging such texts? What risks come from avoiding them?

- How, if at all, does your congregation engage with your Jewish neighbors? What principles should churches follow in relationships with synagogues? How can they ensure these connections help repair the damage of the past rather than do more harm today?

Closing Your Session

Recruit three volunteers to read aloud Matthew 14:28-32, as the narrator (Matthew), Peter, and Jesus. Discuss:

- Why do you think Peter wants to walk to Jesus? Why do you think Jesus grants Peter's request?
- When and how has fear weighed you down in your walk to Jesus? When and how has fear weighed down your congregation?
- Do you share Skinner's positive assessment of Peter's "little faith" (verse 31)? Why or why not?
- "We'll need some hands-on experience," writes Skinner, "out there in the waves, joining Jesus himself in the thick of it all" in order to answer his call to "not be afraid" (14:27). What is your most recent experience of being in chaotic waves of one kind or another as you follow Jesus?
- "Our exploration of Matthew can encourage us to put ourselves among the places and people where Jesus's mercy makes a difference." What next step(s) do you plan to take

to meet Jesus where and with whom he has promised to be, so you may experience his promised blessings for yourself? What next step(s) would you like to see your congregation take, and what can you do to help it do so?

Closing Prayer

Lord Jesus, you command us to follow where you lead, promising you are with us always. Look with favor on us, though we are people of little faith. Grant us such confidence in your power, your mercy, and your blessings that we may live as powerful and merciful blessings to others, especially those who need to experience your blessings most. By your Spirit, may we be the light of the world you call us to be, that all may give glory to our Father, and yours, in heaven. Amen.

Watch videos based on *Matthew* with Matthew L. Skinner through Amplify Media.

Amplify Media is a multimedia platform that delivers high quality, searchable content with an emphasis on Wesleyan perspectives for churchwide, group, or individual use on any device at any time. In a world of sometimes overwhelming choices, Amplify gives church leaders and congregants media capabilities that are contemporary, relevant, effective and, most importantly, affordable and sustainable.

With *Amplify Media* church leaders can:

- Provide a reliable source of Christian content through a Wesleyan lens for teaching, training, and inspiration in a customizable library
- Deliver their own preaching and worship content in a way the congregation knows and appreciates
- Build the church's capacity to innovate with engaging content and accessible technology
- Equip the congregation to better understand the Bible and its application
- Deepen discipleship beyond the church walls